THIS IS A BORZOI BOOK PUBLISHED BY ALFRED A. KNOPF

Text copyright © 2005 by Josephine Poole

Illustrations copyright © 2005 by Angela Barrett

Anne Frank signature copyright © by AFF Basel CH/AFS Amsterdam NL

Random House thanks Penguin Books Ltd. for their kind permission to reproduce an extract from *The Diary of a Young Girl: The Definitive Edition* by Anne Frank, edited by Otto H. Frank and Mirjam Pressler, translated by Susan Massotty (Viking, 1997), copyright © The Anne Frank-Fonds, Basle, Switzerland, 1991. English translation copyright © Doubleday, a division of Bantam Doubleday Dell Publishing Group Inc., 1995. Reproduced by permission of the Anne Frank-Fonds.

www.randomhouse.com/kids

Library of Congress Cataloging-in-Publication Data
Poole, Josephine.
Anne Frank / Josephine Poole ; illustrations by Angela Barrett. — 1st American ed.
p.   cm.
ISBN 0-375-83242-4 (trade) — ISBN 0-375-93242-9 (lib. bdg.)
1. Frank, Anne, 1929–1945—Pictorial works—Juvenile literature. 2. Jewish children in the Holocaust—Netherlands—Amsterdam—Biography—Juvenile literature. 3. Jewish children in the Holocaust—Netherlands—Amsterdam—Pictorial works—Juvenile literature. 4. Jews—Netherlands—Amsterdam—Biography—Juvenile literature. 5. Jews—Netherlands—Amsterdam—Pictorial works—Juvenile literature. 6. Holocaust, Jewish (1939–1945)—Netherlands—Amsterdam—Biography—Juvenile literature. 7. Holocaust, Jewish (1939–1945)—Netherlands—Amsterdam—Pictorial works—Juvenile literature. 8. Amsterdam (Netherlands)—Biography—Juvenile literature. I. Barrett, Angela. II. Title.
DS135. N6F73499 2004
940.53'18'092—dc22
2004015099

MANUFACTURED IN MALAYSIA
August 2005   First American Edition
10 9 8 7 6 5 4 3 2 1

Anne Frank

By Josephine Poole

Illustrated by Angela Barrett

ALFRED A. KNOPF   NEW YORK

I see the eight of us in the annex as if we were a patch of blue sky surrounded by menacing black clouds. The perfectly round spot on which we're standing is still safe, but the clouds are moving in on us, and the ring between us and the approaching danger is being pulled tighter and tighter. We're surrounded by darkness and danger, and in our desperate search for a way out we keep bumping into each other. We look at the fighting down below and the peace and beauty up above. In the meantime, we've been cut off by the dark mass of clouds, so that we can go neither up nor down. It looms before us like an impenetrable wall, trying to crush us, but not yet able to. I can only cry out and implore, "Oh, ring, ring, open wide and let us out!"

Anne Frank, from *The Diary of a Young Girl:* Monday evening, November 8, 1943

The story of Anne Frank begins with an ordinary little girl, someone you might sit next to in class. She had large, expressive eyes and dark, curly hair. She was lively and popular— always surrounded by her friends.

Mostly Anne felt on top of the world. But sometimes she was afraid. There was good reason for this: Adolf Hitler ruled Germany then, and he had vowed to get rid of the Jews.

Anne Frank was a German Jew.

~

Anne was born in Frankfurt on June 12, 1929. From the start, she had plenty to say for herself. She screamed a lot! When little Margot, her sister, peeped into the cradle, she couldn't help laughing. Baby Anne had a mop of dark hair, and her ears stuck out like a pixie's.

Anne's family was lucky. They had money; her father had a job. But for many people in Germany then, life was a bitter struggle.

Germany was blamed for starting the First World War and had to pay huge amounts to make up for all the destruction. It was a harsh punishment. Ten years after the war ended, Germany was desperately poor.

Too many people were out of work. Many hadn't enough to eat. And everyone knew how rich and powerful Germany used to be—one of the greatest nations in the world. So the Germans felt more and more angry and disgraced. They wanted someone to blame—and that was when things began to change, in ways that were frightening for Jews.

There was a man called Hitler—a stiff little man with a mustache—he talked a lot and made big promises. Huge crowds gathered round him. They had no jobs, no hope. No wonder they cheered when he promised to make Germany rich and strong again!

Hitler hated Jews, and he didn't care how many lies he told about them. Who was to blame for all Germany's troubles? Hitler had the answer. He accused the Jews of grabbing the best jobs, snatching the bread from the mouths of workingmen. And it wasn't fair, because Germans were special—the finest race in the world!

So more and more people came to listen, and to vote for Hitler's Nazi Party. It was no threat to begin with—no more than a spark. But the spark was to turn into a flame, and the flame into a blaze that would consume the whole of Europe before it was put out.

There were plenty of ways of making Jews feel unwanted and afraid, even when they were very young.

At school, children began to notice who was Jewish. Some of them mocked and even bullied their classmates. It was very bitter for the Jewish children, to be pushed around and called dirty names by boys and girls who had been their friends.

Soon they would have to sit in a separate corner of the classroom.

It was worse in the grown-up world. People stopped talking to their Jewish neighbors. Jewish shops had their windows smashed. Jews were harassed in the street, even beaten up by the young thugs Hitler called his storm troopers. If they tried to defend themselves, they were rounded up and sent away.

At first, the Jews were bewildered by all this hatred. Soon they were scared. Many left Germany, and Mr. Frank was worried about his family. He found work in the Netherlands and an apartment for them all in Amsterdam that wasn't expensive.

Anne stayed with her granny during the move. She joined the family on Margot's eighth birthday. What a surprise! There sat little Anne, perched like an elf on top of Margot's presents!

The building where the Franks
lived had a garden. All the children
in the block played there on fine days,
practicing handstands, hiding in the
bushes, roller-skating, and skipping
along the pavement. When they wanted
to call out their friends, they didn't
knock on doors or ring doorbells. They
whistled a special tune—only Anne
couldn't whistle, so she had to sing
instead.

One wintry morning she was taken
to her father's office, where she met his
assistant, a woman named Miep. Miep
helped Anne to take off her little white
fur coat and gave her a glass of milk.
She showed her how to work the
typewriter. Anne was exactly the sort
of clever little girl Miep wished to
have herself!

Miep couldn't know that one day she
would stand between life and death for
the Franks, but she loved Anne at once.

Anne and Margot went to different schools. That was lucky, because Anne was naughty in class—not a bit like her hardworking sister! She liked nothing better than telling jokes and pulling faces, so that everyone, even the teachers, burst out laughing.

The girls' friends loved going home with them, for Mrs. Frank cooked the most delicious treats. But if Mr. Frank joined the party, he was the star! He always had a funny story to tell or a game that he'd just invented. All the children adored him.

But no one could forget Hitler's hate campaign. By this time many German Jews had fled to Amsterdam, and Mr. and Mrs. Frank listened anxiously to the grim stories they told—of relentless bullying and camps where people were imprisoned and forced to work for the Germans.

Now Hitler's mighty army was on the move. Britain and France declared war, but the German troops swept on. Soon the Dutch were watching, powerless, as German soldiers marched through Amsterdam.

Once more the Jews were ruthlessly bullied, and the Dutch people soon learned that it was dangerous to stand up for them.

Every Jew older than six was ordered to wear a big yellow star with *Jood* printed on it. Even small children could now be stopped from going into public places like parks and cinemas and swimming pools.

Anne loved going to the cinema. Now she wasn't allowed in anymore. She had to make do with her collection of celebrity pinups—her postcards and snapshots. Nobody would bother to take *them* away!

It was too late to escape to another country. And things could only get worse.

Mr. Frank worked in a tall old building on a canal. Some of the upstairs rooms at the back were empty. Little by little, cautiously, secretly, he moved furniture and provisions into this annex and had a toilet and sink installed. If the Germans had discovered him and his brave Dutch helpers, the punishment would have been savage.

But all went well. Now he was ready for a crisis. It was not long in coming.

Margot was sixteen. One summer day in 1942 a letter came, ordering her to leave home and report for labor service. That meant working for the Germans. Probably her family would never see her again.

They had to disappear, fast. Anne and Margot were told to pack any treasures they couldn't bear to leave behind. With a thumping heart, Anne stuffed her most precious bits and pieces into her satchel—schoolbooks, letters, a comb and curlers, but first of all the diary she'd been given on her last birthday. She squashed everything in with clumsy, trembling hands.

Early next morning she struggled into several sets of underwear, two pairs of stockings, a dress, skirt, jacket, raincoat, stout shoes, a cap and scarf. It was the only way to carry her clothes—any Jew with a suitcase looked suspicious.

They left the apartment with the beds unmade and dirty dishes in the sink, and a scrap of paper with a false address scribbled on it, to mislead the neighbors. Anne had to say goodbye to Moortje, her dear little cat. She cried most bitterly—for who could tell if they'd ever meet again?

Miep was waiting for them in Mr. Frank's office. Quickly, silently, they followed her down a long passage, up a wooden staircase, through a gray door. It led into the secret annex.

Anne looked around in astonishment. Her father had organized all this—thought of everything—and never said a word! But, oh, the muddle! Cases and boxes and piles and heaps—Mrs. Frank and Margot simply collapsed on their beds at the sight, worn out with all the panic and excitement. So Anne and her father set about to put things straight.

From that morning, day after day, week after week, they must keep themselves hidden away. All the time the building was in use, they must stay quiet as mice in the annex—they couldn't so much as run a faucet or flush the toilet. They were in constant danger of being spotted and reported to the police. How they longed for Miep's visits after the workers had gone! She was always cheerful, with news of what was going on, bringing papers and books to pass the time and bits of shopping.

Having to be silent all day—that was almost unbearable for someone like Anne!

The church clock nearby was her comfort. It chimed every quarter of an hour, reminding her that there was still a world outside where children went to school and played together and weren't terrified of being seen or heard.

Another couple moved in with their son, Peter. Now there were seven people hiding in the cramped annex—eight when they took in one more. No wonder they got on each other's nerves!

Anne was the youngest and she suffered the most. She was clever and imaginative, nervous and sensitive, and her growing up would never have been easy. Now she felt she was blamed whenever anything went wrong, while nobody criticized Margot. She loved her father more than anyone, but even he sometimes found fault with her, and that she couldn't bear. Often she cried in bed at night.

She desperately needed someone to talk to, someone who would understand. Not Margot, and not Peter, who was lazy and spoiled—she didn't like him at all at first. She turned to her diary, her diary of letters to "Dearest Kitty," a girl she had known long ago. Now she wrote down even her most private thoughts, because Kitty would never read them, so she couldn't tell tales. The little book was the closest of secrets.

She described life in the annex, the squabbles and dramas. She wrote about her love of nature, which for her was just the piece of sky and the top of the chestnut tree outside the attic window. She wrote about terror—panic terror.

And her feelings for Peter changed as she grew older. She began to understand him. As they became fond of each other, she wrote about love, and hope.

When the little book was full, Miep brought her more paper.

Each evening everyone crept down to Mr. Frank's old office to listen to the radio. Sometimes Anne went to the window and peeped between the curtains. It was odd looking out at the people on the street—as if she were invisible, in a fairy-tale magic cloak. They all seemed so hurried, so anxious—and their clothes were so shabby. Still, Anne was dressed like a scarecrow herself, and there was nothing she could do about that!

Germany was losing the war. After dark, waves of bombers passed overhead on their way to destroy German cities. The night sky throbbed with their sullen roar. If the annex was bombed, everyone inside it would die.

But by now Anne was—almost—in love with Peter. She was happy sitting beside him in the attic, with the comfort of his arm around her. They talked about what they meant to do after the war—or sometimes just sat without speaking while another day passed and the light slowly faded from the sky. It was a love as sweet, and as fragile, as the flowers on the chestnut tree outside the window.

Perhaps, now that the war was nearly over, the people in the annex weren't quite as careful as they had been. Because somebody noticed something and gave them away.

Somebody claimed the blood money the Germans paid for every Jew who was caught.

Now came the nightmare.

Now the smash, crash of a break-in. Boots on the stairs—rough men in uniforms with pistols. They were trapped—there was nowhere to run, nowhere at all to hide.

And soon the sudden space, the light and air—shocking to people who had been shut in for more than two years.

On August 4, 1944, the eight refugees were taken away. The annex was raided and ransacked.

When Miep went upstairs on that terrible evening, she found everything in chaos. Anne's diary was scattered across the floor. Miep collected it and hid it in a drawer, hoping against hope that the family would come back.

But Mr. Frank was the only one to return after the war. He had been separated from his wife and daughters. He knew that his wife was dead. He prayed for good news of Anne and Margot.

Alas, they had died of typhus in a German concentration camp. When the bad news came, he went into his office and sat down at his desk. He felt utterly alone. He had nothing left.

But Miep remembered the diary. She found it and took it to him. She said, "This is for you— from your daughter Anne."

Anne Frank was no more than a girl, and her short life had come to an end.

But her story was just beginning.

What happened to Anne's diary after the war?

Otto Frank was encouraged by friends to publish Anne's diary, and 1,500 copies of the first edition, called *The Secret Annex*, were published in the Netherlands in June 1947 by the Dutch publisher Contact. In 1950 the first translation of the diary was published in German, and in 1952 English translations were published in America and the United Kingdom. In 1955 a stage version of *The Diary of Anne Frank* was performed for the first time, and in 1959 the first film based on the diary was made. The house where Anne hid for over two years opened as a museum in 1960, and it holds Anne's original diary. Nearly a million people visit the Anne Frank House every year. It can be found in the center of Amsterdam at Prinsengracht 267. The contact details are:

Anne Frank House
P.O. Box 730
1000 AS Amsterdam
The Netherlands

Telephone: +31 (0)20 5567100
Web site: www.annefrank.org

Today Anne Frank's *The Diary of a Young Girl* is one of the most widely read books in the world. More than 25 million copies have been sold worldwide and it has been translated into more than sixty languages.

Chronology

1918
November 11 — Germany signs the Armistice (a peace agreement) in Compiègne, France, ending the First World War.

1920
April — The German Workers' Party (founded on January 5, 1919) becomes the National Socialist German Workers' Party, or NSDAP. The term "Nazi" is short for the German *Nationalsozialismus* (National Socialism).

1921
July 29 — Adolf Hitler is introduced as Führer of the Nazi Party (he receives 543 votes in his favor and only one against).

1925
May 12 — Otto Frank marries Edith Holländer in Aachen, Germany.

1926
February 16 — Their eldest daughter, Margot Betty, is born in Frankfurt am Main, Germany.

1929
June 12 — Anneliese Marie (Anne) is born.

1930
September 14 — The Nazi Party becomes the second-largest party in the German Parliament after winning 6 million votes in the German elections.

1932
July 31 — The Nazis receive 37.3% of the vote in the elections.

1933
— The Hitler Youth and the League of German Girls are officially established as youth organizations for boys and girls between ten and eighteen.
January 30 — Hitler is appointed Chancellor of Germany.
February — Freedom of speech is suspended by the Nazis.
March — Dachau, the main concentration camp for political prisoners, is built.
April — The Gestapo (secret police) is established.
— The Nazis declare a boycott of Jewish businesses and medical and legal practices. A law excluding non-Aryans removes Jews from government and teaching positions.
May 10 — Books by Jews and political enemies of the Nazi state are burned in rallies throughout Germany.
July 14 — Hitler bans all political parties except the Nazi Party.
Summer — The Franks decide to leave Germany; the girls stay behind with their grandmother in Aachen, and Otto Frank goes to the Netherlands.

December — Edith and Margot move to the Netherlands.

1934
February — Anne joins the rest of her family in the Netherlands.
August 2 — Hitler combines the offices of president and chancellor and becomes "Führer and Reich Chancellor," abolishing the position of president.

1936
March 7 — The Germans march into the Rhineland (a demilitarized zone on the border of France) and occupy it.

1938
March 12 — The Germans invade Austria.
November 9–10 — *Kristallnacht* (Night of Broken Glass): Jewish businesses and synagogues are looted and destroyed in Germany and Austria by gangs of Nazis.

1939
March 15 — Germany occupies Czechoslovakia.
September 1 — Germany invades Poland.
September 3 — Britain and France declare war on Nazi Germany.

1940
May 10 — Germany invades the Netherlands.

1941
February 25 — Strike in Amsterdam against Nazi brutality toward Jews.
June 4 — Freedom of movement for Jews is restricted in the Netherlands.
June 22 — Germany invades the USSR (Operation Barbarossa).
July 16 — Otto Frank's assistant, Miep, marries Jan Gies, a social worker and member of the Dutch underground.
December 7 — Japan attacks U.S. naval base at Pearl Harbor, Hawaii.
December 8 — United States declares war on Japan.
December 11 — Germany declares war on United States.

1942
January 9 — Jewish children are forbidden to attend public schools and high schools in the Netherlands.
June 1 — Jews in the Netherlands are made to wear a yellow Star of David.
June 12 — Anne's parents give her a diary for her thirteenth birthday.
June 14 — Anne's last birthday party.
June 30 — The Nazis impose an 8 pm curfew on all Jews in the Netherlands.
July 5 — Margot is summoned for labor service.

July 6 — The Franks escape to the secret annex.
July 15 — Germany begins deportation of Dutch Jews to the Auschwitz-Birkenau concentration camp in Poland.
September 15 — Jewish students are barred from attending university.

1943
— Allied bombing of German cities intensifies throughout the year.
February 2 — German forces surrender at Stalingrad, their first major defeat.

1944
July 20 — Hitler narrowly escapes assassination.
August 4 — The annex is raided by the Security Police after an anonymous telephone caller betrays the people in hiding.
August 8 — The Franks are sent to the transit camp at Westerbork.
August 25 — Paris is liberated by the Allies.
September 3 — The Franks are sent to Auschwitz in a sealed cattle car. It was the last transport to leave Westerbork.
September 4 — Allied troops enter Brussels.
October 6 — Margot and Anne are transferred to the Bergen-Belsen concentration camp in Germany.

1945
January 6 — Anne's mother, Edith, dies in Auschwitz-Birkenau.
February/March — Anne and Margot die of typhus in Bergen-Belsen within days of each other.
April 30 — Hitler commits suicide in Berlin.
May 7 — Germany surrenders.
June 3 — Otto Frank returns to Amsterdam, where he is reunited with Miep and Jan Gies.

1947
June 25 — 1,500 copies of the first edition of Anne's diary are published in the Netherlands by the Dutch publisher Contact.

1953
November 10 — Otto Frank marries Elfriede Geiringer-Markovits and settles in Birsfelden, Switzerland.

1957
May 3 — The Anne Frank Foundation is established in Amsterdam.

1960
May 3 — The house where Anne and her family hid for over two years opens as a museum.

1980
August 19 — Otto Frank dies, aged ninety-one.